No Destination

A TRAVELLER'S WAY

SELECTED POETRY BY JOHN MICALLEF

Printed in Victoria, Canada

National Library of Canada Cataloguing in Publication

Micallef, John, 1923-
     No destination, a traveller's way / John Micallef.
Poems.
ISBN 1-4120-0454-3
     I. Title.
PS3613.I23N6 2003   811'.6   C2003-903083-0

TRAFFORD

This book was published *on-demand* in cooperation with Trafford Publishing.
On-demand publishing is a unique process and service of making a book available for retail sale to the public taking advantage of on-demand manufacturing and Internet marketing. **On-demand publishing** includes promotions, retail sales, manufacturing, order fulfilment, accounting and collecting royalties on behalf of the author.

Suite 6E, 2333 Government St., Victoria, B.C. V8T 4P4, CANADA
Phone   250-383-6864   Toll-free   1-888-232-4444 (Canada & US)
Fax   250-383-6804   E-mail   sales@trafford.com
Web site   www.trafford.com   TRAFFORD PUBLISHING IS A DIVISION OF TRAFFORD HOLDINGS LTD.
Trafford Catalogue #03-0823   www.trafford.com/robots/03-0823.html

10   9   8   7   6   5   4

While this is my father's book, it is also in many respects mine and my siblings' book. In this context my brothers and sisters and I dedicate this book to:

Our father, John, for so honestly and so eloquently describing his journey, which is also our journey;

To our mother, Maria, without whose strength, compassion, courage and love the journey would never have begun;

And finally to our Aunt, Margaret, who was an integral part of this journey and who taught us how to love openly and honestly.

Gabriella Micallef

ACKNOWLEDGEMENTS

A special thank you to our Auntie Margaret, my father's sister, who has always loved and supported us through our many endeavours.

The idea for this book came from my mother, Maria, who always saw the beauty in my father's poetry. Thank you for being so persistent.

Thank you to my siblings, Joe, Margot, Rico, Vince and Ivana, who supported this project and helped bring this book to life.

This book was brought to fruition through the dedicated work of Arielle Dylan, who edited the work and provided invaluable insight and Debbie Douglas, who read through all the various drafts of the manuscript and gave meaningful input. I thank them.

Gabriella Micallef

Table of Contents

Introduction

Acknowledgement

INTRODUCTION

No Destination: A Traveller's Way is a collection of poetry spanning six decades. It is my father's work. When I started this project I thought this was a gift for him. After immersing myself in over 1000 pages of his poetry, I was acutely aware of my feelings – past and present. I recalled incidents, stories, memories with joy, anger, guilt, surprise and discovery. Does everyone close to a poet feel the work at this intensity? I realized then that this gift was mine.

My father has written for as long as I can remember. He lived his life as Rilke prescribed,

> "[Ask] yourself in the most silent hour of your night: must I write? Dig into yourself for a deep answer. And if this answer rings out in assent, if you meet this solemn question with a strong, simple 'I must,' then build your life in accordance with this necessity; your whole life, even into its humblest and most indifferent hour, must become a sign and witness to this impulse."

He continues to write today as he approaches his eighth decade.

This collection speaks of journeys: journeys made, journeys regretted and journeys hoped for. It speaks with courage and honesty. It speaks what I know will be difficult for some to hear.

The work is shot through with themes of longing, hope and despair. The first poem, "Sunset of Hope," sets the tone and begins a journey of yearning and desire. The entire selection continues with the journey motif and functions as an invitation to witness the struggle of the human condition, to seek ourselves in others, and to find our value. In all three sections of this work, loneliness,

the fear of (God's) abandonment and pain, is a recurring existential theme, a familiar human reality. But these disquieting poetic representations are balanced with phrases of deeply expressed love and serenity, where profundity and the extraordinary are palpable through insightful treatment of the ordinary. This transformative quality coupled with a gift for strong resonant metaphors is the heart my father's poetic artistry.

The poetic voice of the traveller in this selection of poetry touches the traveller in each of us, that human part that longs to venture forth seeking and yearning for happiness, satisfaction, love and belonging.

I invite you to take this journey.

Gabriella Micallef
Spring, 2003

Words are always getting conventionalized to some secondary meaning. It is one of the works of poetry to take the truants in custody and bring them back to their right senses.

Yeats

Section I
1951 — 1964

Sunset of Hope

Steel bird flies on through mass of clouds,
Under canopy of sky lit by silver flames,
As we chase the sun suspended in the west,
About to set, but never set.

It draws the dark away from our path,
As we rumble to our destination
In the scarlet glow.
We fly through the endless day,
On this trip through this endless land of pioneers,
The measure of my hope,
As I chase the dark,
When hope a glimmer in the night of my despair,
Shines through again, for ever
And ever.

Love

Love is a breeze on a summer day
To refresh the mind in torpor.
Love is a drink on a winter night
To sharpen my will to live.
No love of man or woman,
No love of earth
Can put an end to anguish.
My heart is not mine, Lord,
Keep it, make it your shrine.

Delusion

In mournful moments far from home,
I sought a friend to find relief.
Now at home, loneliness wears out my will,
As I pace through my room
On my empty day, and wait for the night.

Dread

Chains round my will, a weight on my heart,
The claws of dread tear at my hope.
Panic holds my mind and a shroud
Hides my soul.
My hands are tied,
For the hawk of despair preys on my sanity.

Conflict

Mad with frustration, worn out in agitation,
Racked by confusion, harassed with vexation,
With head bent down and clumsy gait,
I search for seclusion
And brood in my solitude.
My whims contradict my will,
So I choke my spleen in indolence.
I seek for peace in books,
But books are dumb.
Doubt gnaws at my mind.
This conflict has sapped my will.

Labour

For long I tried to still the moans of labour;
Now I writhe in pain, as I give birth to my genuine self,
Conceived over and over in lonely rooms,
In lonely houses, in lonely lands,
In a lone mad embrace with my being-in-death.

Ode to Loneliness

I am a discarded dress,
Once the pride of the wardrobe of a bride,
Once the envy of millionaires' wives
Now a rag.
I'm a tangled knot: I cut.
The string comes out in bits –
Loose ends that have no end:
A picture of my life –
All beginning and no ends,
All plans and no results.

I'm a shipwrecked sailor on the rocks
Battered, bruised, bearded.
A crowd of curios come to peer
Like I were a prehistoric fish
Washed on the beach,
Then drive back to their whisky and their jazz
And forget I am.

I am a man alone surrounded by people
As real as shadows, as dumb as statues.

Separation

I envy the breeze in your curls,
The books on your shelves
The walls of your home;
They share our presence:
The sea is separation.
Will love make it disappear?

Longing

I scan the horizon from the edge of the cliff,
While I cling with one hand to a rock,
Shade my eyes from the glare,
As I peer beyond the expanse of the sea.
My foot burns as it stands for hours on the sea;
The crag cuts my skin – my backbone broken.
Yet no funnel looms past the curve of the sea
To announce the news we both dread.
How long do I wait on the edge of the cliff,
While the wind cuts my flesh,
The cold seeps through my bones?
Press the months into weeks,
Cram the days into hours; make time run,
Shrink with desire to hasten that instant of rapture,
When we meet and we greet and we love
At first sight.
Then we both find happiness.

Desire

I wish to crush you in my arms until your
Flesh begins to ache with love, and yearns with pleasant
Pain to feel my flesh, while both my blood and yours
May touch to make the nearness which we feel so sweet
Merge into oneness, cut off from all the world.
So when you possess me, you will find yourself,
For I am your conscious self, the thoughts you dare not think.

I want you in my arms, your flesh on mine, that for one
Fleeting moment lost in time, I know that you are mine –
That you belong to my own flesh and blood.
Your flesh is charged with beauty, beauty that gives joy;
I want to share the thrill of magic charm in your embrace,
The quiet rapture of the silence of the night:
The only witness to our bond of love.

How I Love You

Do not be frightened of my love for you, darling.
My love for you is born in understanding, not in shame.
Not sudden, not absurd, for the heart is not hemmed in by time,
But feels in one small moment the passion of a year
And the gift of heart to heart.

I proclaim my love before the world without a blush,
For my love brings joy to both of us,
Brings joy to all who love me: you are part of them.
You are a sister who lived afar, so far I never hoped
I'd ever meet you. Now we've met: you cannot fade
Into the past to be absorbed by time and memory.

Waterloo Bridge

Time now stands still in a world at peace
That stares on the rippled mirror of the river,
While the earth is wrapped in dreamy sleep.
Then with a roar in the dead of dark
The train thumps, throbs as it rumbles behind
Fast to crash the still and slothful night.

Secret Love

Our love sometimes seems too great, too overwhelming:
It can't be true; it's just a dream, a foolish dream
That you and I have met and found each other.
Yet it is true, so very true that my body
Aches to scream for joy that all the world may know
That we are happy. You've made me happy.

Yet I am afraid: the world would sneer at our love,
And laugh it off as something cheap and silly.
We must keep our love to ourselves, and guard
Our secret from the tongue of gossip and the lash
Of scandal.

Desolate

I am distressed and desolate, empty and alone,
Without a purpose, if I have lost you,
Lost you forever.
I am so tired, tired, trying to clutch at hope.
Desperate I grasp the empty air,
Because you are not there.
Don't ever run away from me and give me back
My loneliness.
Don't ever run away, for now that I have found you,
To lose you means despair.

Anguish

So many years of anguish in patient hope
Have I endured, until I found myself in the woman I love,
In intimate communion.
My peace is short lived.
I am plunged back into my dread.
Once more I am alone, confined into my solitary terror,
Left with no power to fight.
I wait, but I cannot undo my evil,
While time may relish my torment.

No, I cannot destroy the past;
That recent past, so full of hope and mockery
Now haunts my days to come, and demands
Payment for years.
In anguish I will pay.
I will keep on paying until I have the strength
To suffer, while I die bit by bit,
As I prolong a senseless life.

Tears

I have tried to make you happy:
For years I have waited in agony to share your life,
I taught you to love me beyond yourself,
Beyond the love you've always known and cherished.
Now I destroyed all my love, perhaps forever.
So all my words of love have turned to lies,
Or worse than lies – just empty words,
Words to while away the empty hours.
Now my love is only tears for you,
Tears that cannot wash the past away
And give you back forgetful happiness.
The past now haunts you once again:
It haunts us both.
Perhaps it drives us wide apart,
For now we live in fear.

Fancy

I dread to think of you, fancy,
Child of my moods and restless mind.
I yearn to roam with you
Across the world in search of truth.
The truth hid deep within my heart, I miss,
For dreams have filled my mind.
Will then the dream of love come once to life
Before I die? Perhaps I yearn to wander
Through the wide wide world with you,
The symbol of my restless soul
The sigh of a secret longing
And a dream of discontent,
The torment of my heart.

Combat

I wrestle with fate or with failure?
With chance or with destiny?
I am locked in combat with self,
Exasperated with desire of death,
Broken with fury of frustration,
Taut with oppression of tension,
Tamed with dope of hope.
I do not seek to achieve, but to arrive
Faithful to your demands.
What do I want?

Section II
1965 – 1980

Hope

Gently take it in your hand.
Pick it.
Hug it.
Does it seep through your fingers
Like water?
Not again, no.
Let it soak your heart.

Knots

My mind is tied in knots of contradiction,
Knots that strangle my thought,
Entangle my mind in its struggle for release,
While I fritter my time,
Splinter my energy
In routine occupations.

Thanks

For the anguish in my discouragement,
And the confusion in my mind,
The loneliness,
As I piled my notes, stacked my quotes,
Crushed with the vanity of my ambition
Tortured with my helpless isolation,
As I tormented my brain with words,
Stuck in the keys of my typewriter.

Thanks be to God.

Burnt Out

I am burnt out.
The ashes of my dreams stick in my throat;
The smart of smoke pricks my eyes,
While time, like the books on my shelves,
Lies idle in my hands,
As impotent as my brain.

Out the Window

I look out the window on to a world in time,
A whirl of nerves as I sit back on my couch of relaxation.
I think and wait in my detachment
To come out of my timeless cell into the crowd,
To shake some sleepy man out of his dream.

Yet I must wait, while a ripple of voices
Reaches to my room,
Like a waltz of the sea caressed by the wind.
The world may slide out of its orbit,
Crack, blow up like a midget star,
Scatter its debris into the nothingness and vastness of space.

I wait, as I plan my work,
Wait for the moment and the occasion
That define my life.
I wait, while I look back
And see the myriad paths I trailed
To nowhere,
Crossing and crossing again
To a dead end.
Yet I turn in the dark and strike another trail.
Obstinate in defeat?
Or too proud for failure?

No Signposts

I stand at the crossroads and look:
No signposts point to a destination.
No landmarks tell the roads.
The roads are gone.
The desert encroaches on the land,
As I wander across the dunes
Of my despair.
My destination is survival,
Not arrival.
I am no pilgrim.
Just a tramp.

Barrier

I do not reach your grief across the barrier of estrangement
That soars between our minds, keeps us apart,
Though our bodies touch in an embrace of melancholy,
As we clutch at love in a gesture of despair,
For desire is drained through days of anger.

Have we lost contact? With our bodies close,
Yet no words bridge the gap between us,
Distant, two strangers lost in a maze of delusions,
Condemned by a mass of mistakes?

The Philosopher

Opening the windows of the mind,
So you can look beyond the expanse of time and space,
And see the hidden God, the sun of truth,
Rising out of the mist and emptiness of the dawn.

Eighteen

How slow the years have moved out of the lanes
Of time, and now – now they are yours
To live, enjoy – but now they run
And leave you old, grownup and sad.

Do not grow up, my girl. Push back the eager
Years and live your days in slow slow motion,
Forgetful, like a child that time creeps on
Through the wrinkles of care and your fear of tomorrow.

Expo Montreal

Girls with wide trouser legs,
Women chic in their dresses,
Kids with sweaters slung over their hips,
Arms tied up on their tummies.

Split

My day is split into before and after –
Before nurtured with hope that the letter comes,
And after sad with disappointment slowly moves
Into the next before and merges
Into the never-ending after,
As I wait and wait, and then – still wait;
But I no longer know if it's before or after.
Before and after are the same.
Before and after I wait – I wait in my agony.

The Land

Straight road through the valley,
Nestling me like a womb,
As the land with its hills,
Like a many-breasted mother,
Goddess of spring, and fertile virgin,
Priestess of hope;
But my mind is far away, my heart sick
As I think of people I love, and feel
The desolation of my heart.

I see the beauty of the land,
And feel my work is sterile,
My words as dry as summer fields,
And your heart locked up in a barren love,
As barren as my words, my useless words.

Patience

I've slowed down my life to a standstill;
But life goes on, and life has passed
Me by.

I feel like a fool manipulated by fate.
Am I learning to be wise,
As I yield to people's wishes
For the sake of peace?

Contact

The search for words –
Words to reach out and touch the distant heart,
The heart that feels, but finds no words
To tell the anguish that wears out hope,
The hope that gives the courage to endure
Till death.

But the words are silent,
And the heart is dumb,
And the hope dead,
And the people I love so distant;
So distant, yet so near I hear their voices
In the next room.

Section III
1981–2003

Sing Again

If we bared our souls, as we looked eye to eye
And felt free from fear, then words
Become a balm for bruised minds,
And balsam for hurt hearts,
And we begin to feel alive,
And perhaps once again
You begin to sing,
And I perhaps remember how to laugh.

No More Stars

Do you grudge me the wine I drink
To help me cope with my solitude?
I do not see
The stars shining from my window.

Recognition

How beautiful is the world with its blossoms in spring,
Or the fruit in summer, or the scatter of leaves in the fall,
Or the snow mantle of winter.
I do not recognize the season I live through.

SoundScape

Voices in my head, voices in the store,
Clanging of dishes in the house, rush of traffic in the street.
The stars are far away.
The stream murmurs like women at prayer.

Only the Fear

Only the fear of life remains,
Like a hidden pain stabbing at our heart,
And turning our silver years into a drudgery.

So now I question, but find no answer.
I cease to ask, and accept the fact:
I do not know how to come closer.

Voices

My children are happy this Christmas,
This silver anniversary of our wedding;
But my life is shot, shattered, a heap of ruins,
Like a mound of earth over my grave,
As I strive to crawl out and reach up
And grasp an anxious hand,
And come back to life,
And share my children's joy,
As I listen to their voices this Christmas.

Surfacing

Schemes and temptations surface in my mind,
And circle through whorls and eddies in a frantic
Attempt to force me into action; but my heart
Is paralyzed with hesitation and scarred with doubt.

Courage Lost

I've lost the courage to defy the fate
That thwarts my resolution to persevere till I complete
What I set out to achieve: fear grips
My heart to give up this endless struggle,
And tempts me to drift into a blanketed withdrawal.

Hand of Death

One day, perhaps I felt
The clammy hand of death,
As it touched your face.
My words so unexpected
Broke the barrier of my silence.
I've rarely told you
How I feel, perhaps;
But I've always looked up to you,
And loved you so much,
So very much, my brother.
But I never said the words.

Sheath of Silence

Voices and laughter in a whirl of joy
Reach into my cell, and suck me down
Into a vortex of solitude,
As I feel like a misfit dumped at random
In the basement or forgotten in the attic.
Handy in need but out of the way,
Safe and useless in my sheath of silence.

The Search

Condemned to this routine by my bigoted belief
In my brains, I plod through the weary tramp
Of life, tempted to let go,
And drift in the stream of time
With its capricious moods,
Or rush through the lure of the new
And try to feel alive,
As I let my ups and downs
Run my day.

Direction

The wish to die, the urge to live long
And work hard at writing
The dread of a shelf of manuscripts
Gathering the dust of futility in my closet,
Makes my life a useless toil.

Tear at my heart, beat on my brain,
And make me yearn to fade out of existence,
Not like a coward scared to face his life,
But burnt out like a candle.

Life is a celebration of joy and gratitude
For the gifts received, but disregarded as redundant,
For the achievement is considered more important than
    the experience
And life prolonged into a useless chore.

Silent Words

The words repeated over and over,
Telling again and again the incidents
We shared and the joy stalking our desolation,
And the memory stabbing our joy at your absence.

The words like a tangle of gossip,
Repeated over and over, as we remember
The joy we felt, but your memory warped,
As we stifle our tears and quash our memories.

The words don't fill up the void
Of your absence through the empty house in the night,
As we try to laugh to fool despair
With our simulated fun and forget you're gone.

Through the drab hours of the idle wake
We find no comfort in words,
No comfort in memories, no
Comfort in tears, as we sheathe our memories.

Our sorrow in my silent words, as I stifle
The loneliness the words take shape
In my head, but my voice remains choked in my throat.

Locked

Why have I locked my soul in this cell of solitude
To strive for the achievement that eludes my soul?

Dissatisfaction

Now I read, but rarely write.
I feel lost, as I flirt with my books,
Searching for the truth, a shadow in the dark.

My eyes are dim, as I peer into the night,
And my mind, in dread of the ghosts that creep
Out of the cracks of time and scare my hope away,
Strays into a lane of dissatisfaction.

Deliverance

Like a patient I accept this body of hesitation,
And yield to my mind in doubt, as I put up
With the fear in my heart, yet still I strive
To hope in the mercy of my Lord, and trust
In his forgiveness, while I endure these chains that bind
My body in hesitation, tied up in knots
Of doubt that pull my heart tighter,
Oppressed by the fear that haunts my mind.
I question the will of my Lord,
Yet I know I can find deliverance only
If I let go, while I strive to put up
With the anguish in my soul, the seal of my humanity,
And trust in the compassion of the heart of Christ,
Even if I shudder as I try to understand.

Humdrum – Summer

This humdrum roll of humdrum days
Drags on through a tunnel of boredom, as I wait
For a spark to set my mind on fire,
And make my heart glow with passion,
And burn with flames of inspiration. Alas!
This summer of drought dried up my mind,
And choked my heart with suppressed wrath,
And silenced the ripple of laughter in my tomb
Of dread, where I lie immured behind a wall
Of dusty books and yellow folders.

Humdrum – Autumn

My mind is strewn with the withered leaves
Of the autumn of my thoughts, curled and dried
And dead; while the throb in my head, like the growl
Of a hound, cracks my skull like the crumbled
Filigree of yellow leaves burnt out
In the arid oven of my useless passion,
And my heart, drained of the sap of satisfaction,
Crackles in the heat of my sterility and yearns
For the rain of inspiration to soak my imagination
And reach out for roots into the dirt of life.

Humdrum – Winter

My mind is bare like a skeleton tree,
While the wind of wrath rages in my heart,
And the storm of passion drives me crazy
With its temptation to ignore the shelter of my shell
Of patience, and crawl out of my cave of hibernation,
And ski across the virgin snow of life
Over ridges of obstacles and crevasses of danger,
Through the screen of my words,
Down the face of the mountain of adventure,
And hit the open road of freedom.

Humdrum – Spring

My heart yearns for the spring, turgid
With hopes like swollen udders, to blossom
Forth into a rose romance, and bring
Back joy into my heart with the thrust
Of love. Alas! I'm trapped in the snare
Of right and wrong, locked in my cell
Of faith, chained in my dungeon of despair,
Committed to endure my loneliness in a straitjacket
Of impotence, or break my word, and twist
My life with guilt of love fulfilled.

My Way

I used to know. I used to walk
And know where I was going; but now the road
Curves, twists into an abrupt end.

My mind, orphaned with care, strays
Into a wilderness of doubts that oppress my heart
And mock my commitment to my futile work.

I torture my soul with my search for whys
And puzzle my wife with cryptic words
That hide their meaning, as I reach out for understanding.

I end up with a riddle for an explanation, as I confuse
My mind with my attempts at justification, while doubt
Tears at my soul, widowed by anguish.

The ground breaks up, and I cling to the roots
Of my resolution, suspended in an abyss of dread.

Control

Like a dying man who takes too long to die,
Yet knows he soon must die,
So waits for death to seal his fate,
I've stopped fighting for control.
Perhaps this jumble is a dream:
It does not matter,
For soon I wake up, master of my mind,
And this tangle of thoughts fades out into a blur
Of memory, and leaves me with no desires – dead.

Let me enjoy my pride without qualms of guilt,
My Lord; or cleanse my heart from regret,
And teach me to endure my failure;
But close my heart to temptation and despair,
In this agony of frustration, as I wrestle my way
Out of this labyrinth of terror,
My prison of anguish.

Presence

You tantalize my expectation with the awe of your surprises,
And flutter my heart with a storm of passion,
You charm my pen with the lure of insight,
As I soak in the bath of your flamboyant presence.

Your presence triggers a rhapsody of thrills,
And blows my mind into a trance of passion,
And I feel my life grooving in so tight
You leave no room for questions.

Then, so often you force me to long
For the day you go away; but when
You are gone, I try to evoke your presence
With my regret to chase away your absence.

Your presence has become the torment of my heart,
But your absence freezes my soul dead.

ISBN 141200454-3